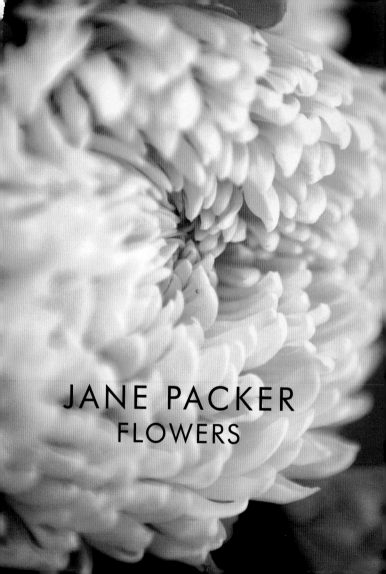

JANE PACKER
FLOWERS

JANE PACKER
FLOWERS

BEAUTIFUL FLOWERS
FOR EVERY ROOM
IN THE HOUSE

with photography by
Catherine Gratwicke

RYLAND PETERS & SMALL
LONDON • NEW YORK

CONTENTS

INTRODUCTION

This little book showcases an array of floral arrangements that are genuinely easy to achieve yet are also creative and inspiring. Flower arranging doesn't have to be complicated, so don't worry about following rules or needing special skills. All that's required is some imagination, an eagerness to experiment and an ability to see beyond the norm. These arrangements are truly simple and straightforward. Better still, they use easily obtainable blooms and all the flowers retain the signature Jane Packer style.

Not everyone has a big budget for flowers. Clever choice of containers can result in some fantastic effects and allow you to use fewer blooms. In this book, you will see vases clustered together with flowers popped into only one or two of the containers. This creates a feeling of abundance and celebration, despite using only five or six stems. If the amount of flowers in some of the arrangements seems extravagant, then save them for special occasions and remember that just a few beautiful stems arranged in the right way can also make an amazing impact on your home.

Look with fresh eyes at the containers you have at home. Beautiful flowers don't require heirloom crystal vases. Often the unexpected – a tea caddy or old umbrella stand – excites the most comment and admiration. Fresh flowers should make you happy, and if they make you smile too, then so much the better!

BUYING, CONDITIONING AND REVIVING

If you choose flowers carefully and look after them well, they will give you pleasure for longer. This process starts in the flower shop, where following a few simple pointers will prevent you from spending money on wilted flowers that only last a day or two. Make sure that all the flowers on the stand have their stems in clean water. Avoid any with soft, floppy heads or petals that are starting to brown at the edges. Stems that are shedding leaves will also be past their best. Cut stems will brown at the site of the cut – an indication that they've been hanging around for a while. Look for flowers with pert heads and some stems still in bud. Leaves should be firm and a fresh green colour (not yellowing).

Conditioning cut flowers

Sometimes flowers are not given enough water, so they need a long drink to quench their thirst. When you get them home, re-cut the stems at an angle to enlarge the surface area – this will enable more water to be taken up. Remove any foliage from the lower part of the stem to help keep the water clean. Now plunge the flowers into a deep container of water. If there's a sachet of flower food attached to your blooms, use it. Whether you have purchased a bunch of flowers or a single rose, the rule is the same – change the water every day and the flowers will last longer.

Conditioning bouquets

If you are lucky enough to be given a beautiful bouquet, the same rules apply. Using sharp scissors, trim all the stems on the diagonal, only taking off a small amount (otherwise you may spoil the proportions), and remove any foliage that lies below the water line. Don't cut the twine holding the bouquet together, otherwise your lovely arrangement will simply fall apart.

Reviving floppy heads

If they are left out of water for too long, many flowers will start to hang their heads. However, there is a way to revive them. Take several sheets of newspaper and lay the stems on top. Now tightly roll the paper around the flowers so that any drooping heads are held upright. Re-cut the bottom of the stems at an angle and stand the flowers in a deep container of water for several hours, then unwrap them. The blooms should be beautifully upright. If hydrangeas or roses look a little tired, the whole heads can be plunged into a bowl of cold water to revive them. In general, misting flowerheads with water will perk them up and, if done every day, will increase the longevity of your flowers.

DESIGN PHILOSOPHY

The Jane Packer design philosophy is very simple: the inspiration is nature and the way flowers grow on the plant. A signature Jane Packer bouquet or arrangement is limited to one colour, often in a range of tones, and includes no more than three or four different varieties of flower. The result is simple, beautiful arrangements that never look stiff or contrived.

Balance and harmony

When it comes to arrangements, the aim is to balance flowers and container to create a harmonious whole. A decorative vase should be paired with simple flowers while a dramatic display needs a container that won't compete. The traditional rule of using an odd number of flowers in an arrangement still stands, as this results in a more naturalistic composition.

Vases and containers

If you enjoy flowers, build up a collection of containers of different shapes and sizes. A tall vase is right for long-stemmed flowers, while a low tank works best for table-top arrangements. A classic flared shape needs a large quantity of flowers to fill its mouth, so works well with inexpensive blooms such as narcissus. And dainty bud vases that hold just one bloom give great value for money.

FAVOURITE FLOWERS

Although nowadays you can source many flowers all year round, at Jane Packer we try to use those that are in season. There are a few wonderful 'luxury' flowers that still only appear for a few short weeks every year, such as peonies or lily-of-the-valley. Such blooms can be obtained out of season, but they tend to be very expensive and often the quality isn't very good. Many of these flowers have a very short vase life – stocks or lily-of-the-valley, for example. Just enjoy them as a fleeting pleasure and don't expect them to last, or you'll be disappointed.

Roses are the signature Jane Packer flower and epitomize luxury and glamour. Roses are beloved of florists for many reasons. They are reliable, long-lasting, available in ever-bigger sizes and make a great focal point for any arrangement. The wedding market is enormous and new roses are developed to meet the demand every year. The trend at the moment is for scented roses that resemble blousy garden varieties for a romantic vintage feel.

There are many robust cut flower varieties that will last a week or more and so offer great value for money. Chrysanthemums and carnations, for example, are tough as old boots. They may not be particularly special, but the secret is to buy and arrange them en masse to make an impact. Other long-lasting blooms include lilies, proteas, calla lilies and gladioli.

HALLWAYS

Overlooked and underloved, the hall or entryway often tends to be a rather neglected area of the home. Fresh flowers will bring this space to life and create a warm welcome.

Hallways are frequently cluttered and even scruffy, home to discarded shoes, coats, umbrellas, bicycle helmets, junk mail and all those other household items that haven't yet found a home. At the same time, they are a high traffic area, with children, family, friends, pets, delivery services and tradespeople all coming in and out. They are first and foremost practical spaces – something to bear in mind when you are adorning them with flowers.

Having said this, the entrance hall is one area of the home that cries out for fresh flowers. After all, first impressions count, and you never know who is going to pop in for a visit! Scented blooms in the hallway will greet you with their evocative perfume as soon as you step through the front door. Lavender, sweet peas, peonies, Paperwhite narcissus and hyacinths are all good options.

Halls and entryways vary greatly in shape and size, so make the most of the space you have available. If your hallway is wide enough for a shelf or a narrow console table, this is the perfect platform for fresh flowers. A console can be adorned with an assortment of interesting vases in different colours, shapes and sizes. These vases make an attractive display when empty and look even better when filled with flowers.

A narrow, corridor-style hallway is often dominated by a large staircase at one end. It is easy to complement this style of hall by placing a large vase of flowers at the foot of the stairs. Choose a tall, slender vase and fill it with structural flowers such as gladioli, arum lilies or delphiniums; elegant, tall-stemmed blooms that echo the strong verticals of the stairway

If you are lucky enough to have a large entryway, you can really go to town with flowers. A substantial vase arrangement on the floor, a table or placed to the side of a chair can make a bold statement, but don't forget that a bud vase containing a single exquisite specimen flower and positioned on a side table can have just as much impact. If you have the space, opt for both!

It's fun dressing the hallway for a special occasion, whether it be a wedding, a homecoming or a summer party. And at Christmas time, you have every excuse to deck the halls, introducing glossy evergreen wreaths, aromatic garlands of pine and perhaps even a Christmas tree, depending on your space. However, you don't really need any excuse to introduce fresh flowers into your home, and the entrance hall offers the perfect opportunity to showcase your personality and welcome guests with open arms.

OPPOSITE Statice is a flower that all but disappeared from smart florists. However, it is becoming popular all over again, due to its longevity, delicate flowers and huge range of colours. Statice is low-maintenance and dries well; it's guaranteed to brighten up even the darkest of hallways.

ABOVE These lemon-yellow mophead hydrangeas may appear completely natural but they are in fact dyed. Hydrangeas are great value – two or three heads clustered together can make a statement. The densely petalled heads look so fabulous that they work beautifully arranged alone.

ABOVE AND OPPOSITE A mass of red and green dendrobium orchids is casually arranged in a tall ceramic vase. The lime green and chilli pepper hues make for a bold and unexpected colour combination. Dendrobium orchids are especially long-lasting, which makes them good value for money. You'll be able to tell they are near the end of their life when the flowers start to delicately fall from the stem.

OVERLEAF These shapely blooms of fiery lipstick-red amaryllis bring a touch of heat and drama to a narrow mirrored chest in a cool white entrance hall. The arrangement is very simple, but using two identical vases in different sizes doubles the impact.

OPPOSITE A narrow white hallway is brought to life with colourful flowers. The staircase has been dressed for a summer wedding or party with an array of flowers in dazzling hues.

THIS PAGE Cut from the garden, these graceful spires of white lysimachia seem to mirror a swan's white plumage.

OPPOSITE Velvety claret-coloured gladioli and purple cotinus leaves are a punchy combination against the tomato-red stairs and vase. Not for shrinking violets!

ABOVE This elegant composition combines oak leaves that have been dyed vibrant purple with delicate red skimmia cut from the garden. The low, urn-shaped vase is classical in style, but set against a matt black wall the display takes on a modern feel that suits the space perfectly.

KITCHENS AND DINING SPACES

You don't need tons of flowers to dress a kitchen, and you don't need show-stopping arrangements. Fill the kitchen with simple, unpretentious flowers that you will enjoy every day.

The best thing about flowers in the kitchen is that they can be relaxed and informal; this is not a traditional spot for floral displays, so no-one has high expectations. This allows you to play around with fruit and berries as well as flowers – think rosehips and chilli peppers, or a huge bowl of artichokes with their intriguing furry texture. If you have a garden, bring in flowers, foliage or blossom-strewn boughs. Trailing lengths of ivy can decorate a long table, while branches of apple blossom look striking in a tall vase.

In the kitchen, it's fun to use containers that give a nod to their surroundings. Search your cupboards for kitchenware such as tea caddies and coffee pots, or wash out and reuse glass food jars or tins. Enamelled jugs are the perfect home for a sheaf of tulips, and you can pop a dome-shaped posy of sweet williams into a colourful glass sundae dish. Vintage coffee cans are the ideal receptacles for velvety anemones or a single luscious camelia, while jelly moulds or copper pans can be filled with a mass of small-headed roses. If you're arranging flowers and end up with a broken-off bloom, pop it in a shot glass, place it by the sink and contemplate its beauty as you wash the dishes.

The obvious place for kitchen flowers is the table. Keep it simple. A long table allows you to have a row of small arrangements dotted along its length. A round table is well suited to a central arrangement, but remember not to make it too tall, or it will interrupt the flow of chat. Sideboards and dressers can also play host to flowers. Place smaller arrangements where they can be enjoyed at close quarters – on a shelf, perhaps, or on the counter alongside a pile of cookery books and the wine rack.

A separate dining room is less common nowadays, but if you do have one, the dining table calls out for flowers. They will bring the room and the table to life, and delight your guests. However, the days of stiff centrepieces built on florist's foam are long gone. Keep the flowers informal, interspersed with twinkling candles. If you have a long table, it's nice to have flowers at intervals along its length. Try three identical vases each holding a low bunch of different white flowers. Alternatively, go for a mismatched row of glass bottles each containing a single stem of the same flower. But avoid strongly scented flowers on the dining table – any chef will tell you that they can be offputting when food is being served.

PREVIOUS PAGES In this cosy family kitchen, different shades and textures of red and white bring life and interest to the kitchen table and echo the cheerful gingham cloth. Small jugs and a large decorative food tin hold a variety of blooms, including an enormous fluffy protea head dyed a vibrant red, a cluster of delicate crimson nerines, glossy rosehips and tall stems of shiny red chilli peppers.

LEFT This little colony of comical penguin jugs is just the thing to bring fun to the kitchen – they look as if they're gathering round for a chat. The penguins are filled with plants that will last in a hot, steamy kitchen environment, as they live on the moisture in the air

ABOVE AND OPPOSITE Everyone who sees these unopened allium seedpods is entranced by their sculptural good looks. The acid lime colour is so dramatic and striking against the kitchen blackboard, and the sleek stems, bulbous pods and smooth, almost rubbery surfaces throw into relief the rough wood of the chopping board, the sleek stainless steel and the textural ridged vases. Alliums are members of the onion family, which makes them a perfect choice for the kitchen.

THIS PAGE Although the delicate
dill seed heads and the sprays of
unripe blackberries on this shelf are
not intended for consumption, their
culinary connections mean they
work perfectly in a kitchen.

ABOVE Pompon chrysanthemums have been tucked into a vintage enamel coffee caddy. The way in which the flowers have been tightly grouped is quite a modern concept, yet the container is of times past, showing how a mix of old and new can work brilliantly together.

OPPOSITE This is such a playful use of a vintage coffee set. The white thistle peeps out of the top of the pot like steam rising from hot coffee. Quirky ideas like this are a good use of flowers that won't fit into a larger arrangement or stray blooms that have outlived other flowers.

PREVIOUS PAGES Silver-backed senecio leaves, veronica, astilbe and white astrantia are used to adorn a collection of vintage milk bottles.
OPPOSITE AND ABOVE Amazing textures make for amazing bouquets. This lush hand-tied bouquet contains Majolica spray roses, creamy white hydrangeas, vibrant green poppy heads, and white-painted bear grass.

THIS PAGE AND OPPOSITE These pure white 'Mont Blanc' amaryllis are absolutely stunning with their glowing green centres. Here, they are arranged in two layers for a contemporary feel that suits the surroundings. The display emphasizes the smooth green stems and the large white flowers.

The cloudlike bloom of the white
hydrangea flower is quite ravishing
in close-up. Use it with other white
flowers, or gather an armful for
a dramatic vase display.

THIS PAGE Garlands look wonderful winding along a table, snaking in and out of place settings, glasses and candles. This example has a blowsy charm that makes it perfect for a tea party.

ABOVE This arrangement is quite traditional in terms of the container and the composition, but has been brought up to date by massing the flowers together into a compact dome shape. It combines full-headed white roses with smaller-budded white spray roses, hyacinths and astrantia.

OPPOSITE Blue on blue. These delicate Scabiosa reward closer inspection, thanks to the exquisite detailing on each fragile flowerhead.

THIS PAGE AND OPPOSITE All the colours of the rainbow appear here, and in such bright, sunny tones too. Each vase contains a tight posy made up from different flowers that are all the same colour and hue.
OVERLEAF This mass of summer flowers in blues, purples and cerise makes an imposing centrepiece. It's a classic composition of scented delphiniums, stocks, peonies and roses; all country garden favourites. The arrangement has been made with florist's foam to hold the flowers in position and ensure a long life, so it will need to be watered daily.

THIS PAGE The daintiest sugar-pink hydrangea floret nods shyly over a tonal bud vase. Pop it by the sink and contemplate its beauty as you wash the dishes.

OPPOSITE Celebrate spring with a jugful of purply pink-hued tulips. Tulips are thirsty flowers, so keep them topped up with water.

ABOVE Stems of perfect white peppercorns tumble over the edge of an urn-shaped vase. Seen against the surrounding smooth white ceramics, the peppercorns don't appear white at all but take on a rich sepia tint.
OPPOSITE The faded ice-cream shades of these roses work so well with the dull metal of the champagne bucket. A higher binding point on the arrangement means that the flowers are massed together more closely.

LIVING ROOMS

One of the quickest ways to make a living room feel special is to use flowers. They remind us of the natural world, the changing seasons and the planet that we live on.

A living room may be large or small but, whatever its size, it should be a space that makes everyone in the family feel relaxed and comfortable. The best living rooms always appear cosy and welcoming, no matter what season it is. We often choose to accessorize with cushions, lamps and other bits and pieces, but it's flowers that truly bring a living room to life.

When it comes to choosing flowers for the living room, first consider your space. It's important to select blooms that coordinate with the other colours in the decorative scheme. Next, think about the opportunities for flowers within the room – could your mantelpiece be brought to life with a bowl of gardenias, for example? Coffee-table arrangements are perennially popular, as they make a good focal point. They are usually designed to be seen close up or from above, and as such they lend themselves to single-flower arrangements of intricate flowers such as dahlias, roses or hydrangeas that invite close inspection. Large fireplaces are the place for bold floor-standing displays in statement vases that make an impact and draw all eyes. Go to town with armfuls of delphiniums, gladioli or amaryllis.

Don't neglect other areas – bookshelves, mantelpieces or side tables will all be enlivened by the addition of flowers. Use a table lamp to spotlight a bud vase holding a single rose, or cluster a group of vases of the same colour on a console table then fill each one with peonies. Sitting rooms often play host to a work or study zone squeezed into a small corner, and flowers can make such a space a pleasure to spend time in. A posy of sweet peas beside the laptop will certainly cheer you up as you file your tax return.

If you love entertaining, one of the quickest ways to dress the living room for a party is to use seasonal flowers. In springtime, fragrant blooms add an extra dimension – think of the heady perfume of hyacinths and narcissus. Also available at this time of year are branches of blossom, pussy willow or sticky bud, all of which can create dramatic displays while offering good value for money. If you are lucky enough to have an ornamental fruit tree in your garden, saw off a couple of branches and bring them indoors for a breath of spring.

By summer, you'll be spoilt for choice. Seasonal favourites include hydrangeas, peonies, roses, pinks and stocks, many of which also have the benefit of scent. Summer flowers – stocks, for example – are not always long-lived, but their fast-falling petals only add to their evocative allure. By autumn, ring the changes with dramatic foliage arrangements. And in winter, go for berries, glossy evergreens, architectural amaryllis and ruffle-edged brassicas.

THIS PAGE Bud vases have a narrow neck that's designed to hold just one or two blooms. The choice of flowers is obviously important – this sculptural modern example is perfect for showcasing tall, dramatic flowers.

OPPOSITE Eucalyptus pods are pale in colour with a beautiful silvery lustre that here is complemented by the bark wrapped around each container.

OPPOSITE AND ABOVE This is a spectacular display of a jumbo variety of stachys, otherwise known as lamb's ears. Soft to the touch and with an intriguing woolly texture, it's irresistibly strokeable. The huge white silver birch vase gives the arrangement even more presence.

OPPOSITE AND ABOVE We take for granted the warm flames of a fire in winter, but when it comes to the summer months, the fireplace is a dark, empty space – the perfect opportunity for an imaginative arrangement. Encased within glass cloches and a large jar sit vivid green hydrangea heads. Viewing the flowers through glass makes them feel like botanic specimens and by enclosing them they become a precious item.

ABOVE Lime-yellow button dahlias have been cut to different heights and used to fill a cluster of exotic brass vases on a low table.

RIGHT An armful of tulips that are still in bud spills lavishly out of an old brass lantern. With tulips, you need to re-cut the stems and change the water daily, as they carry on growing in water.

THIS PAGE AND OPPOSITE This design is very contemporary in style, thanks to its feeling of calm simplicity and the streamlined shapes of the containers. The lower vase contains smooth poppy heads all in a row. The taller vase holds three vibrant green sweet williams; delicate and fluffy, and in complete contrast to the smooth surface of the poppy heads.

ABOVE These tuberoses are simply divine. Their waxy white flowers can be slow to open, but release an amazing scent when in full bloom. Here, they are in tight bud, so have a lovely lime green tinge.
OPPOSITE Sunny yellow eremurus stems reach up to a metre/three feet in height and are studded with tiny flowers that slowly open from bottom to top.

THIS PAGE This arrangement postively exudes old-fashioned glamour. The scent of gardenia flowers is amazing and will fill a room, taking your breath away with its seductive quality. Surrounding the blooms is a mass of glossy foliage. Gardenia plants have a rarity value in the northern hemisphere, as they are native to a much warmer climate.

THIS PAGE Dainty white pompon chrysanthemums have been cut short and arranged in a low bowl. They are available all year round, are inexpensive and have a long vase life.

OPPOSITE This huge glass fishbowl vase is filled with white hydrangea. It may look as if only a few stems are required, but appearances are deceptive and you will need 10 or 11 heads to fill a bowl of this size.

OVERLEAF Peeping over the top of each tiny antique boot is a dainty white aster with a bright yellow centre reminiscent of a garden daisy. The asters are the perfect size, and will keep fresh for at least a week.

LEFT White arum lilies are truly classic but have a contemporary feel, thanks to their sleek, architectural good looks. In this economical yet very effective arrangement, five long-stemmed arums have been divided between three similar vases of varying heights. Note how the flowers have been arranged to fall in different directions to give interest and structure to the composition.

As well as having a flawless, Art Deco-style elegance, arums are robust flowers and should last for at least a week in a cool area. However, the stems are fleshy and prone to making the water murky, so it's advisable to change the water every day.

THIS PAGE This arrangement of clustered purple-blue hydrangeas and hyacinths gets its impact from the restricted colour scheme and the oversized column vases. It's a real attention grabber

OVERLEAF These cornflowers, also known as bachelors buttons, are an almost unbelievably vivid, saturated electric blue. They are not expensive flowers yet used en masse, as here, cornflowers can create an outstanding presence.

THIS PAGE The vibrant deep-blue hue of gentiana is its greatest asset, along with the way the trumpet-shaped flowers are studded along the length of the stems. Gentiana are well suited to tall, narrow vases such as this one, and due to the generous number of flowers on each stem, just one or two can create a dramatic effect.

OPPOSITE A vaseful of powder-blue delphiniums reaches for the sky, surrounded by a ruffle of similarly hued hydrangeas, which add volume and depth. The curvy vase echoes the silhouette of the lamp behind.

THIS PAGE These amazing architectural flowers are actually globe artichokes – yes, the ones you can eat! The heads are extremely heavy and are best contained within a vase with a narrow neck and heavy base so that they are well supported.

RIGHT Feast your eyes upon the amazing hues in this small head of hydrangea. Each purple petal has an electric-blue centre and veining, leaving a dreamy trail of vibrant blue, pink and red.

PREVIOUS PAGES Red alert! This is a painterly arrangement of three different kinds of red dahlia, including a variegated variety with intricately detailed petals that seem to have been dipped in white paint.

ABOVE The Black Baccara rose is a deep, luscious red that's almost verging on black. Here it's paired with red amaranthus, stripped of its foliage to prevent the leaves detracting from the magenta flowers.

OPPOSITE Celosia is one of the most intriguing cut flowers. Arrange it in a low vase so that you can appreciate the fluffy texture and the intricate whorls of the flowerheads from above.

ABOVE AND RIGHT These luscious rich red garden roses have been casually arranged to suit a relaxed modern interior. The arrangemement may be simple but it's also immensely sophisticated and pairing the roses with a glossy red vase doubles their impact.

OVERLEAF LEFT More roses. The lush, densely petalled heads of this rusty red variety have an old-fashioned, vintage feel.

OVERLEAF RIGHT With their exotic, otherwordly beauty, dark pink vanda orchids make an unusual ceramic vase into a focal point.

THIS PAGE Don't dismiss vintage vases or containers – they can bring humour and panache to a contemporary backdrop. These two elephant containers are making stately progress along a shelf. The smaller of the two holds classic red roses – a complete contrast to the wild eucalyptus with its dramatic foliage and bright red seedpods.

OPPOSITE Glorious bright orange dahlias have been tied into a perfectly domed posy and popped into a retro leopard-print vase. The arrangement is a true scene-stealer, sitting proudly between two 1930s-style chairs reminiscent of old-fashioned cinema seats.

ABOVE These globes of orange tulips and chrysanthemums would make a bold statement on a reception desk or as party centrepieces.

THIS PAGE AND OPPOSITE
Chocolate cosmos are such
a sumptuous deep red that they
appear almost black. These
delicate flowers are not
long-lasting but their fragility
makes them even more special.

BEDROOMS AND BATHROOMS

Waking up to fresh flowers is a real joy, so indulge yourself. Floral arrangements aren't just for show and have just as much of a place in the private corners of the home.

We're used to seeing floral arrangements in hallways and living rooms, but people don't always think of putting flowers in the bedroom. It's a shame, as even a tiny posy on the dressing table allows you to revel in the beauty of flowers close up.

Bedroom flowers should be glamorous and indulgent, just like the choice of blooms shown in this section. Allow your yearnings for romantic, feminine blooms free rein, and choose luscious roses, feathery astilbe, ranunculus, sweet williams or lily-of-the-valley. Enjoy a bowlful of blowsy garden roses on your dressing table or place a tiny bud vase of delicate, jewel-like muscari or hellebores on the bedside table/nightstand. And don't forget the subtle charms of old-fashioned cottage-garden favourites such as peonies, cosmos, sweet peas and violets.

Flowers in a guest bedroom create a hospitable effect. A floral display on a bedside table/nightstand looks particularly appealing, even if it is just a single hydrangea head in a glass tumbler. Add a glossy magazine, a carafe of water and a couple of glasses for a boutique-hotel effect. If feminine flowers aren't your style, or if you are entertaining male houseguests, opt for orchids – they are sculptural and elegant without being too boudoirish.

Bathrooms offer the perfect opportunity to use strongly scented flowers, such as hyacinths or narcissus. In a guest bathroom, pair them with scented candles for a luxurious spa effect that will make guests feel indulged and pampered. Exotic flowers also work well in this room, as their strong, clear colours pop against white sanitaryware or tiles – think of lipstick-red gloriosa lilies, a sheaf of gladioli or orange kangaroo paw.

Bathrooms are also a friendly environment for house plants, especially those that love humidity, such as orchids. If you revel in heady scents, opt for gardenias or stephanotis, which will both thrive in warm, humid conditions. There's a huge array of decorative succulents that would also do well, such as crassula, sempervivum or echeveria. If you struggle to keep your house plants happy, try moving them to the bathroom – you may find that they flourish in the moist conditions.

If you're entertaining guests, remember a little posy for the downstairs bathroom – again, scented flowers would be nice, but just a single graceful stem in a bud vase is enough. Add a thick pile of hand towels and a scented candle as a finishing touch.

THIS PAGE AND OPPOSITE
Feminine elements work well
in a bedroom and these two
arrangements – one of veronica
(opposite) and the other ranunculus
(this page) are perfect examples of
this. Veronica is an excellent choice
if you want something inexpensive
and long-lasting.

ABOVE These phytolacca berries are amazing. Just look at the bright lipstick-pink stem and mass of glossy lime-green berries. Phytolacca berries are toxic when raw, so this is an arrangement that's best avoided if you have inquisitive children or pets.

RIGHT Feathery astilbe looks so delicate but is actually quite robust and will last over a week. Here it is used en masse, leaving the foliage on the stems to add volume and contrast to the arrangement.

OPPOSITE This soft pink bouquet consists of roses, celosia, snowberries and pink bouvardia individually wrapped in glossy aspidistra leaves.
ABOVE Never pass an antiques or vintage store without having a rummage for pretty containers. Here, red skimmia cuttings fill a pearlized pink vintage vase that sits proudly beside a ceramic bambi. Skimmia has small, berry-like buds that last for quite some time.

ABOVE Lustrous purple protea heads are intriguingly tactile. They are tough and longlasting in arrangements, as proteas are designed to withstand the enormous heat of their native growing conditions.

OPPOSITE You might expect to find delphiniums in all shades of blue, but these dreamy lilac spires are something of a departure from the norm; the flowers range from regal purple to palest lavender. You don't need to do much to delphiniums – their loose, country-garden style is perfectly suited to simple arrangements like this one.

PREVIOUS PAGES A lavish arrangement of zesty lime-green summer flowers: molucella, pompom-like guelder rose and a wide collar of 'Limelight' hydrangeas – a fairly new variety with a froth of fine petals.

OPPOSITE AND ABOVE This tall arrangement is a striking addition to a minimal bedroom. Twiggy lilac branches are adorned with sprays of phalaeonopsis or moth orchids. The waxy white flowers really do look a little like a cloud of moths fluttering away from the branches.

PREVIOUS PAGES A retro-style vase holds amber-yellow leucospermum nutans combined with sunny yellow chrysanthemums, dark-berried eucalyptus, pale pink veronica and hot pink gomphrena.

OPPOSITE A touch of bold colour pops against the neutral tones of this bathroom. The large vase holds fiery orange crocosmia, while orangey yellow leucospermum nutans pop like firecrackers out of the small vase.

ABOVE This white china toothbrush holder has been put to a new use as a vase for single stems of vibrant orange asclepias.

ABOVE A dainty and demure green hellebore in a curvaceous ceramic bud vase is the perfect adornment for a downstairs cloakroom.

OPPOSITE This old-fashioned ceramic shell has been filled with heads of white sedum. It should last a few weeks even in a steamy bathroom.

OVERLEAF This emerald-green bathroom is home to a wide range of succulent plants, ranging from tiny aloe vera to large, round-leafed crassulas. Succulents are ideal plants for the bathroom, as they can live off the moisture in the air and will need very little watering.

OPPOSITE In this simple bathroom, an armful of stocks stand in an old galvanized metal milk pail. Imagine relaxing in a foam-filled bath with the wonderful sweet yet spicy scent of the stocks filling the room.
THIS PAGE Spring-flowering paperwhite narcissus are another perfectly scented flower for the bathroom. They exude a potent and delicious perfume that is out of all proportion to their tiny size.

UK SOURCES

Jonathan Adler
60 Sloane Avenue
London SW3 3DD
+44 (0)20 7589 9563
*Whimsical, quirky and
luxe homewares including
a fabulous range of
ceramic vases.*

Alfies Antiques Market
13–25 Church Street
London NW8 8DT
+44 (0)20 7723 6066
www.alfiesantiques.com
*Huge and eclectic range
of collectables, including
unique vintage glassware
and ceramics.*

Abigail Ahern
12–14 Essex Road
London N1 8LN
+44 (0)20 7354 8181
www.abigailahern.com
*An eclectic yet sophisticated
collection of furniture and
decorative objects.*

Amara
www.amara.com
*Browse a huge offering of
vases from international
designer brands including
Tom Dixon, House Doctor
and littala.*

Bodo Sperlein
www.bodosperlein.com
Ethereal, magical ceramics.

The Conran Shop
Michelin House
81 Fulham Road
London SW3 6RD
+44 (0)20 7589 7401
www.conran.co.uk
*Cutting-edge designs,
including clear glass vases
in different shapes and
sizes, as well as quirky
Perspex containers and
chunky ceramics.*

Debenhams
www.debenhams.com
*A wide variety of vases
in all sizes and shapes,
part of the Designers at
Debenhams range.*

Design Nation
www.designnation.co.uk
*This website promotes
British design and
showcases the work of
young ceramicists and
glass designers.*

Designers Guild
267–277 Kings Road
London SW3 5EN
+44 (0)20 7351 5775
www.designersguild.com
*Decorative glass vases
plus some hand-crafted
ceramics and tableware.*

Graham & Green
www.grahamandgreen.
co.uk
*Vases and containers in
a variety of styles, from
vintage chic to sleek
contemporary styling.*

Habitat
196–199 Tottenham Court
Road
London W1T 7LG
and branches
www.habitat.co.uk
*Good-value, trend-led
styles, including a selection
of classic glass vases.*

Heal's
196 Tottenham Court Road
London W1T 7LQ
+44 (0)20 7636 1666
*Visit www.heals.co.uk for
details of your nearest store.
Both classic and
contemporary styles.*

Ikea
www.ikea.com
Cheap and cheerful vases, some of which look almost as good as their designer counterparts.

Jane Packer
75 George Street
London W1U 8AQ
+44 (0)20 7935 0787
jane-packer.co.uk
A carefully chosen selection of interesting and unusual vases and containers as well as beautiful blooms, of course.

John Lewis
300 Oxford Street
London W1A 1EX
+44 (0)20 7629 7711
Visit www.johnlewis.com for details of your nearest store.
A good range of affordable glass and ceramic vases, glassware and other containers.

Liberty
Regent Street
London W1B 5AH
+44 (0)20 7734 1234
www.libertylondon.com
Beautiful and unusual hand-crafted pieces.

Nest
www.nest.co.uk
Designer vases and modern planters from design-conscious European brands including AYTM, Hay and Ferm Living.

Pentreath & Hall
17 Rugby Street
London WC1N 3QT
+44 (0)20 7430 2526
Simple and elegant glass vases plus pieces by American ceramic artist Frances Palmer.

Scabetti
www.scabetti.co.uk
Unusual pieces created by designers Dominic and Frances Bromley.

Selfridges & Co
400 Oxford Street
London W1A 1AB
www.selfridges.com
Adventurous designs from a range of designers, including Tom Dixon, LSA, Fornasetti and Alessi.

Skandium
www.skandium.com
Vases by celebrated Scandinavian manufacturers, all displaying the clean-lined Scandi aesthetic.

Vessel
114 Kensington Park Road
London W11 2PW
+44 (0)20 7727 8001
www.vesselgallery.com
The very best contemporary glass and ceramic design, with a strong emphasis on Scandinavian and Italian 20th-century glassware and ceramics.

Vivienne Foley
www.viviennefoley.com
Thoughtful, beautiful pieces in organic shapes.

Zara Home
www.zarahome.com
Good-value vases and containers whose eclectic good looks belie the very reasonable prices.

US SOURCES

ABC Carpet & Home
888 & 881 Broadway
New York, NY 10003
+1 212 473 3000
www.abchome.com
Unusual pieces, including collaged earthenware vases and antique silver over copper 'birch bark' vases.

Jonathan Adler
www.jonathanadler.com
Groovy retro-modern vases and tabletop accessories.

Anthropologie
www.anthropologie.com
Quirky, well-priced vintage-inspired vases and containers.

Brimfield Antiques Show
Route 20
Brimfield, MA 01010
www.brimfieldshow.com
This famous flea market runs for a week in May, July and September every year.

Crate & Barrel
www.crateandbarrel.com
Good basics for anyone starting to build up a 'vase library'.

English Country Antiques
26 Snake Hollow Road
Bridgehampton, NY 11932
+1 631 537 0606
www.ecantiques.com
Period country furniture and decorative accessories.

Fishs Eddy
889 Broadway at 19th Street
New York, NY 10003
+1 212 420 9020
www.fishseddy.com
Pressed glass pitchers in jewel shades and cute toile d'Jouy printed vintage-style ceramics.

Heath Ceramics
www.heathceramics.com
Bud vases in organic shapes and tempting hues.

House & Hold
www.houseandhold.com
Architectural shapes from Danish brand Ferm Living.

IKEA
www.ikea.com
Cheap-and-cheerful glass, ceramic and rattan vases.

Macys
www.macys.com
Vases from Kate Spade, Kosta Boda, Orrefors and Vera Wang.

Mikasa
www.mikasa.com
Classic crystal and stoneware vases plus art glass bud vases.

Pier One Imports
www.pier1.com
Seasonal selection of affordable, trend-led vases.

Ruby Beets Antiques
25 Washington Street
Sag Harbor, NY 11963
+1 631 899 3275
www.rubybeets.com
Holmegaard glass, Italian pewter bowls and rare Chinese porcelain.

Target Stores
www.target.com
Clear glass vases in every size and shape imaginable.

West Elm
www.westelm.com
Good-quality, good-value containers, including brass vases, marbled glass and dainty bud vases.

INDEX

PICTURE CREDITS

Ryland Peters & Small and Jane Packer would like to thank the following home owners who so kindly allowed us to photograph their homes for this book:

Sue Williams A'Court
www.suewilliamsacourt.co.uk

Jo Berryman
www.matrushka.co.uk
joanna@matrushka.co.uk

Chaucer Road/Light Locations
www.lightlocations.co.uk

Victoria Davar and Shane Meredith
Maison Artefact
273 Lillie Road
London SW6 7LL
www.maisonartefact.com
mail@maisonartefact.com

Sarah Delaney
Sarah Delaney Design
www.sarahdelaneydesign.co.uk
+44 (0)20 7221 2010

Charlotte-Anne Fidler and
Matthew Griffiths
www.airspaces.co.uk

Mark Homewood

Page 70 'Tall bird form' ceramic vase by Vivienne Foley (www.viviennefoley.com)

All photography by Catherine Gratwicke apart from the following pages: 1-4, 9, 13, 46-47, 50-53, 60, 63, 70, 102, 104, 109, 120, 132, 141, 144 and endpapers, all by Paul Massey.

Art director Leslie Harrington
Senior commissioning editor Annabel Morgan
Location research Jess Walton
Head of production Patricia Harrington
Publishing director Cindy Richards

First published in 2011 as *At Home with Flowers*
This revised edition published in 2020 by
Ryland Peters & Small
20–21 Jockey's Fields
London WC1R 4BW and
341 E 116th St
New York, NY 10029
www.rylandpeters.com

10 9 8 7 6 5 4 3 2 1

Text © Jane Packer 2011, 2020
Design and photographs © Ryland Peters & Small 2011, 2020

ISBN: 978-1-78879-215-8

A CIP record for this book is available from the British Library.

Printed and bound in China

The original edition of this book was cataloged as follows:

Library of Congress Cataloging-in-Publication Data

Packer, Jane, 1959-
  Jane Packer at home with flowers : beautifully simple arrangements for every room in the house / photography by Catherine Gratwicke. -- 1st ed.
      p. cm.
  Includes index.
  ISBN 978-1-84975-119-3
1. Flower arrangement in interior decoration.
I. Gratwicke, Catherine. II. Title. III. Title: At home with flowers. IV. Title: Beautifully simple arrangements for every room in the house.
  SB449.P2245 2011
  745.92--dc22
                        2010051126